Chronos

Flavia De Luise

My Positano

Co-Author Alessandra Baduel

Translator Stella Fusca

Photo Editor Maurizio Garofalo

© 2023 **Europe Books** | London

www.europebooks.co.uk – info@europebooks.co.uk

ISBN 9791220141697

First edition: September 2023

Distribution for the United Kingdom: **Vine House Distribution ltd**

Printed for Italy by Rotomail Italia

Finito di stampare nel mese di settembre 2023

presso Rotomail Italia S.p.A. - Vignate (MI)

My Positano

NOTE OF TRANSLATION

In adapting Flavia's memoirs into English, we have tried to respect her style, the peculiarities of language and the specificities of the Positano environment, which already distinguish and enrich the original Italian version.

Alessandra Baduel and Stella Fusca

FOREWORD

Telling one's life story is, first and foremost, a way of finding and recognising oneself, even when the protagonist plays the role discretely or, as in this case, tends to shrink in stature like the donor in a Renaissance painting.

The first feeling produced by this memoir lies, then, in what the author, with an attitude deliberately alien from emphasis and rhetoric, tells us about herself, her family, her friends and girlfriends, and her "Positano", genius loci of this story.

Flavia transported me to the beautiful world of my youth and childhood, in which I ended up getting lost between reality and imagination. I realised that storytelling is the most effective means of passing on one's emotions, values and experiences to those younger than us.

With Flavia, we share the *positanesità*. We were born, in Positano, we lived nearby, our moms were like two sisters, and I think that's why Flavia specifically asked me to express in writing the admiration that her family history deserves.

But Flavia's life – and the family to which she belongs – is not quite like any other; we cannot fail to refer to it, to the events of her life, if we want to reconstruct and understand the reality of the culture and industriousness of the Positano that has taken shape over the past decades, and as it appears to us today.

And so, without ever missing the exquisitely human, personal tone, without ever losing Ariadne's thread of subtle amorous dismay, the family novel becomes a historical novel, a lucid, indispensable memory of time.

Virginia Attanasio Cinque
Il San Pietro di Positano

I dedicate these memories to my husband, my family, and love, which beyond the age of eighty remains the only energy I believe in and the thing I wish for everyone.

I was born in this wonderful place called Positano, in the centre of the Amalfi Coast, in August 1940. I lived in a strategic spot, in the middle of the village, at the small stairway between the Sponda descent and the street of the shops, an obligatory passage to go to the sea. After school I would run to the beach, a two-minute walk, and play until evening with my girlfriends.

Among the pebbles on the shore, there were to be collected colourful bits of majolica and glass rounded by the waves – and sometimes you would even find a coral spring. There was the volcano game, typical of our area. We would stock up on matches, paper, and sugar, then make a mound of sand with a hole from the top, 'the pipe', and one on the side to fill it with a small paper wrapping of sugar. One lightened match, and so our miniature volcano made fire and flames – in truth, mostly a bit of smoke.

Another pastime was *mazza 'e pivezo*, bat and rod, which we played in the feet-in-the-water variation. With a stick, you have to blow a small wood as far as you can, then run into the sea, get your feet wet and get back to base before your opponent makes his move. If you succeed, you score an extra point. And there were always the 'wars' between groups: children of vacationers versus those of fishermen, but also those from the Chiesa Nuova against those from I Mulini, or boys against girls. We used to build sort of imaginary kitchens with chalk on the pavement of the promenade next to the beach, or in a narrow street. Having marked the boundaries of rooms and furniture, we would put in some used jars as pots, and of course when everything was ready the boys would arrive to destroy it, out of spite.

I mentioned the children of the vacationers and in fact, after the war, slowly slowly, the village began to become a tourist destination. Not the chaotic and commercial tourism of nowadays, but beautiful people, who had their home and stayed with us for a long time, even at Christmas, New Year's Eve, and Easter, not just in the summer. Writers, painters and musicians, industrialists and entrepreneurs. They came from all the most beautiful cities in Italy and abroad. From Naples we had wonderful families, as from Rome, Milan, and many other cities, with whom there was a relationship of respect and friendship. So it was how my sister Luisa and I, since in 1956 opened our coiffeur at the small stairway next door, had a wonderful clientele.

My adventure began – and I was privileged, in this: I was able to do a work that I enjoyed, and I got to know the whole world, even travelling to perfect myself, but above all because the world came to Positano.

In those years, children's games were made of pure fantasy, such as that of the volcano that made 'fire and flames'. Children of fishermen and vacationers competed on boats at the shore, or on the bronze lions on the beach. Opposite page, a portrait of myself from that time.

And because of our commitment the world also came to us, with ladies of all kinds, always fond and faithful. We weren't even twenty in the beginning, but we were eager to do and learn.

Before our coiffeur, my father, Pompeo De Luise, had a tailor shop there. The aiders were Alfonso Di Gennaro, Pepito, Giovanni, the brothers Salvatore and Vito Fiorentino. Some then launched themselves into the so-called 'Positano fashion' and made their fortunes with a life of great commitment and sacrifices. Alfonso for example created, together with his wife Maria, the "Lampo" tailor shop, and Pepito the boutique with his name. My father instead, stopped being a tailor because, as he said, a man's suit with Zegna and Cerruti fabrics cost forty-two liras: a lot of money in those times, most families couldn't afford it.

He changed his work and was the first to have a cab. We didn't have ambulances in the village at that time, and he was often the one who transported the sick, in particular the little ones, to the Cotugno Hospital in Naples. But beds weren't always available, so my father was the first to practice nonviolent civil disobedience: he would not move from the admittance desk until some doctor, moved by compassion, found a place for the sick little one. During the typhoid epidemic that hit us after the war, being away for work he was unable to bring a 12-year-old girl to Naples in time. No one else had wanted to accompany her, for fear of getting infected, so he took her late and unfortunately, she died on the way, in the car.

He was always busy, with all the entrepreneurs' families coming. For example, Carlo De Angeli Frua, a textile industrialist, wanted to be picked up in Milan to go first to Puglia, where he had land holdings, and then come to his beautiful villa here, up above viale Pasitea. Today it is called Villa Magia. Through him, we also got acquainted with the famous model known as Pinuccia, who had a milliner shop on via Montenapoleone in Milan. Once, the model wanted to go blonde: my sister and I stayed at the salon until midnight. Between her and De Angeli Frua there was a big age gap. He bought her a cute little house in the village, she also came alone. At one point she got involved with a Positanese younger than her, Giacomino *'o Stagnaro*, the tinker. She even took him to Milan.

Some of the most beautiful villas, then, were in the Fornillo area. Until the Fifties, the famous playwright Aldo De Benedetti lived there. In 1940 De Sica shot *Rose Scarlatte* from one of his texts. Being of Jewish descent, since 1938 the playwright could no longer sign his works, due to the fascist racial laws. And for the same reason, that year he moved to Positano, even then homeland of artists and shelter for those in need, long before being a destination for vacationers. De Benedetti stayed throughout the war. There was also Cesare Giulio Viola, writer, playwright, and screenwriter, with his villa where he took refuge writing that ours was *"the village of free men, that is, of artists"*.

The famous small stairway before the opening of our coiffeur.

On the right is my mother, Maria Castellano. Here above, from the right, my father Pompeo De Luise, the municipal engineer, and Vittorio Rianna: son of Pantalione, one of the coachmen of the buggies, he learnt to drive the car with my father and also became a taxi driver. At the top, in the middle of the second row, from bottom, I'm with my eighth-grade class in Amalfi, where we had to go to attend. On the opposite page, me and on the right my friend Mariateresa Collina. Beside again my father and below vacationers on a walk near the beach.

Here beside, my grandmother
Flavia Rispoli, a great traveller,
with her brothers behind her:
on the left Giuseppe, who had
become a priest, on the right
Salvatore, the founder of the
Buca di Bacco. Top left, fisherman Alessandro Di Leva with
his *lampara*, the boat for night
fishing. On the right Pasquale
Castellano. My mother's relative, he had lived in New York
for a long time, we called him
uncle Patsy. Facing page Vittorio Rianna, still a coachman,
before becoming a taxi driver.
It was very nice to go around
the village, slowly slowly, in a
buggy. Valentino, Pantalione,
Barilotto and Peppino were
the coachmen.

In the beginning, fishermen were also boatmen for tourists. At night they went out with the *lampare*, boats with a big lamp, when still part of the village – and the whole Coast – lived on fishing. The dark water was dotted with lights like the sky, a luminous net. In the background, below, the islands of the Galli. It was Marquise Eva de Ruggiero, with her first boutique in Positano, who made me the suit for my honeymoon in 1961. There was also the overcoat because it was January: as not to overlap with summer work, we did all the ceremonies in winter. Opposite page, top on, the wedding day with my husband Michele Della Mura. On the right my friend and client Trude Zeiss, on the left Marquise de Ruggiero and my father. The child is Marianna Rispoli, daughter of Giuseppe. Below, I am at the Rome Zoo. On the right, my dear friend Mimì Collina, owner of the Bar Internazionale.

It was from one of his books, *Pricò*, that the movie *I bambini ci guardano*, still by De Sica, was made. He also participated in *Sciucià* screenplay. And De Sica used to come to visit him, as did many other well-known people.

But about Mrs De Benedetti, there was once a problem, let's say a misunderstanding. She was leaving and my father was accompanying her to Naples. On the way he gave a lift to a housepainter who was going on foot to Piana di Sorrento for an emergency: he had to buy some medicines for his wife, who was sick. The lady become very annoyed. She had not understood the desperation, the need of the poor man.

"Pompeo", she said angrily, "It is me paying for the car, how dare you let another person in?!". My father stopped the vehicle: "Madam, you haven't paid me yet, I'm free to bring whoever I want". And dropped her off with all her luggage. He also had a complaint about this fact. But he couldn't help himself.

Surely, with the cab everything happened, especially in the early years. For example, clients often didn't have the means to pay. And my father, as they say, brought patience. But a unique case was that of the expressionist painter Grigorij Oscheroff, a Russian of Jewish descent who regularly rewarded him with his paintings. One of those paintings still hangs in my house, it was also displayed in a collective exhibition of the painters who lived here.

Pompeo De Luise never became rich, but at his funeral the whole of Positano was there, and also many people from nearby villages: he was renowned for his generosity. The legacy of this side of his character was inherited by Maria, the eldest of the three children I had with my first husband, Michele Della Mura. In addition to working in her mother-in-law Brunella's clothing shops, she has always been in the Red Cross and helps anyone in need. She also worked hard for the removal of the architectural barriers, which are a real problem here.

My mother, Maria Castellano, was also very generous. When the war was coming to an end, some deserters from the Italian army were on the run. Having nowhere to stay, they slept on the small stairway in front of the house. My father was in charge of collecting potatoes and oil in the countryside, that were distributed to the population. So she made potato salads dressed with oil to feed them. One day a German soldier arrived, also fleeing from his army: my parents helped him like the others. *"Song' figl'e mamma, loro non hanno colpa"*, they are mama's boys, they are not to blame, my mother said. During fascism, my father also spent three days in jail for refusing to take the party card. But we had the mentality of those who do not bear a grudge.

When the Germans surrounded the area and were in the mountains, they couldn't enter the village because the bridges had been blown up, but the deserter was very frightened and my father took him to a farmer friend's land, in the Teresinella hills. "Don't be afraid, no one will find you here", he told him.

Every now and then he went to see how he was, but one day he found him lifeless. He had hanged himself. It was a very painful episode. My mother always remembered him, she said he had red hair. And we heard nothing more about an Italian

My father was the first to have a cab in the village, and everything happened to him. But the unique case was that of the Russian painter Grigorij Oscheroff, who paid with his paintings. Above, the works still in our house. The little girl in the sketch is my sister Luisa. Alongside the director Vittorio De Sica in Positano, where he used to visit friends who lived here, like Cesare Giulio Viola.

Mayor Paolo Sersale welcomes General Clark to Positano. That arrival meant a lot to the village. Thanks to the mayor, who obtained the water pipes. We only had borough fountains before. And there was the typhoid epidemic to prove that an aqueduct was very urgent. That was the real start of it all. Also the base camp was established here for Allied officers, who then returned over the years on vacation.

soldier who had left us a suitcase, promising that when he got to his home in Sicily, he would contact my parents to have it sent to him. The suitcase has been in the house for years, in vain.

Once the war was over, the village began to grow. We owe a lot to people like Paolo Sersale and Carlino Cinque for their ability to treat guests with elegance, kindness, and human warmth. I must say that in this we are a special people, everyone has played their part, in fact there is the saying: *"Positanese, amante del forestiero"*, lover of the foreigner.

And there was the great merit of Marquis Sersale precisely, mayor in the first postwar period and later, and of his brother Franco. Back then, we only had neighbourhood fountains. Upon the arrival of the Allies, they explained to General Mark Clark that an aqueduct was urgently needed. The ongoing typhoid epidemic proved it perfectly. It was then that Sersale also thought up a big lie to help the population: he declared that we were seven thousand inhabitants, instead of the actual two thousand. So the pipelines were connected, plenty of water arrived but also rations of flour and food for five thousand more. That was the beginning of everything. Not to mention that the general had the base camp established here for the officers, who then returned over the years on vacation, with their families.

There weren't many hotels: the Margherita, the Roma, the Savoia, the Miramare, the Maresca, the Montemare, the Villafranca. The Buca di Bacco, of my mother's relatives, which was also a bar and nightclub. When there was live music in the evening, we would go down with mum, my sister, and some girlfriends. In addition to the blankets to put on our legs, we used to bring eggplant parmigiana sandwiches.

We peeked through the *séparées* that closed off the terrace to see at least a glimpse of that forbidden and fascinating world. After midnight, from the yachts at anchor would descend Jane Russell, Harry Belafonte, Onassis with his wife Tina Livanos,

The mayor with the parish priest, don Saverio Cinque, around the village and at lunch at the old Caffé Flavio Gioia, which would later become the Buca di Bacco. Below Paolo Sersale again, at the post office.

Opposite here, a *soirée* at the Buca di Bacco in 1962. Sitting together, Sophia Loren and American actress Jayne Mansfield, who also received the Golden Saracen award on that occasion. Above a view of the beach with the stairs and the Buca. Facing page above, Grace Kelly, again at the Buca. Below left, Prince Rainier of Monaco in the village with one of his two daughters. On the right, the rich and whimsical American artist Kimball Underwood, called 'Mister Kim', who lived in Positano for forty years. In the picture he is at one of his famous parties with his wife.

In those years, many vacationers still came by public coach. Then, to get to the hotel or the rented villa, there were buggies, and porters to help them with their luggage up the stairs. Pretty heavy suitcases: holidays were long.

31

The beach with the first cabins and above the church of Santa Maria Assunta. On the right Jayne Mansfield with husband and children. Everyone took pictures because she was a well-known actress, she made her career in Hollywood as a 'rival' to Marilyn Monroe. But many photos were also due to her bikini, which at the time was not so common to see around here.

the Agnelli, and Prince Rainer with Grace Kelly. I still remember how pleasant the feeling of the tepid sand on my feet was. Sometimes we used to bathe, in the middle of the night, in a warm, clean water.

The Buca always had live music with international artists, it probably had been the most famous nightclub on the Coast. But it was a hangout for the whole day. In the evening for the *beau monde*, during the day also for the children of vacationers, who were kept at bay on the beach by lifeguard Pasquale, while perhaps competing with the fishermen's children among the boats pulled ashore. From the Buca started their treasure hunts organized by the mothers and there they would hang the *pignatta*, the crockpot to break blindfolded, or the paper donkey to attach its tail to, always blindfolded. Games like this, made of nothing and fantasy.

The memory of poverty, however, was still there in the Sixties. Once a whale was caught, and everyone gathered to see this huge thing lying out on planks raised by trestles, in the little square going down after the church, where the fishmonger was. Many people helped him slice it that day: yes, they would all have eaten it, the times of hunger were still quite close, the end of the whales was not really thought of.

Gradually, many more hotels opened, as well as guesthouses. La Caravella, down by the sea next to the Buca, was the first residence. An Australian neurosurgeon used to come right there and stayed for a month. It was 1954 when he visited my mother, who was ill. Sadly, in those days there was no cure for brain tumours, so in 1955 she left us.

A short time later, out of necessity and passion, my sister and I decided to open the beauty salon. It was a craft already in the family. My grandfather, Angelo Castellano, had been the only barber in Positano for years. His wife Flavia Rispoli, my maternal grandmother, brought seven of their eight adult children to New York and three of them became hairdressers. When they came back to Italy, in 1948, they brought the first all-metal hair dryer, scissors with long tips, flat stork beaks for hair and the perm to be applied with heat.

That hairdryer lasted for years: my brother-in-law Baldo De Martino, Luisa's husband, fixed it constantly. And when a girl had to get married, she would borrow it to dry her hair. Until hair dryers became a cheap product even in Italian shops, ours made the tour of the village. But it wasn't just about these little things: we were all always helping each other, also with money loans. Those who had earned the most lent to those who were about to start their own business: of boats, premises and rooms to be arranged and rented out. Or there were diseases, problems. The benefits were shared. And in the end, sometimes the money didn't all come back. It also happened with petrol.

My father had opened a fuel pump where the Mulini garage is now, and had to pay the tanker truck on arrival, otherwise they wouldn't unload. From the boats, from the speedboats that were consuming so much, they would come up with jerry cans and: "Then I'll pay you". Recovering wasn't easy, but in the end, better not get bitter blood.

In those years, my mother, some girl-friends, my sister and I, came down in the evening with a sandwich and a blanket. We stood on the sand, peering out from behind the séparées, fascinated at the **beau monde** that gathered at the Buca. Above, the entrance. Below are the La Caravella residence, which was next to the Buca, and the courtyard of Palazzo Murat. Here on the side, the Caffè Flavio Gioia, above the staircase of the lions.

As for us, Luisa learnt how to cut hair and we opened the salon. In the first years, we had a Neapolitan lady to whom we gave 50% of the proceeds to teach us the craft in return. After some time, I went to Naples, to do a L'Oréal school course. Then I did another one in Rome. My sister was getting better and better and so we continued on our own. We took local apprentices and workers from outside, in three years we set up three salons: the first at the entrance to the house at the small stairway, the second at the beach, above the lions, going towards the church stairs, the third near the piazza dei Mulini, a first-floor next to the small cinema that is no longer there.

We had fabulous success, good times, beautiful people, simpler life, but there was elegance and good taste. We were, with the salon at the beach first, a reference point for our clients, their children, tourists also from the rest of the Coast, everyone.

At the time it was Paris dictating fashion, both for clothes and hair: we went to Roger Parà's school in rue Jean Mermoz, next to rue Faubourg Saint-Honoré, where still stands the "Maison de Beauté" of the famous Carita sisters, constantly on the rise with their innovations for hair, face, and body care. Parà was himself part of the parisian Haute Coiffure, he collaborated with names such as Balenciaga, Balmain and Guy Laroche. He had one of the first and most important schools in the branch. The Lido Bluebells acted as models and the teachers explained us the new cuts, colours, and the balayage – which today we call shatush: in my sixty-four years of profession, it all comes back. But thinking about those years, one must also remember Anthony Mascolo. Son of Italians who emigrated to London, with his father, a barber, and three other brothers in the profession, he was awarded best British hairdresser several times between the Eighties and Nineties. He opened schools in London, New York, and Italy. And founded the TIGI group, with products spread all over the world. With them, my daughter Patrizia attended both the Rome and the London schools.

Going back to talking about Paris, in 1968 my sister and I were there for the update and were invited by L'Oréal to the imperial eagles' room of the Hotel de Crillon. At the buffet there were canapés, caviar, champagne and cream puffs. There was also a grand piano with a pianist and a tenor who performed the most beautiful songs, both French and foreign, dedicated to the guests. Since we were from Campania, they sang 'O sole mio. The tenor was of Italian descent and was glad to talk with us, he was homesick for his country. The other participants in the class were all from Northern Italy, looking down on us.

But one day, in rue Faubourg Saint-Honoré a spider stopped, driven by Monsieur Herbignon, the owner of a famous brand of champagne, who of course always came on holiday to Positano. And he, with this most luxurious car and a nice cache-col, hailed us greatly: the others were terribly disappointed.

We also went to the most interesting stores for our work and found both flat and tubular scalpels, rosewood sticks and bristle brushes. All unobtainable things, in Italy. When I came back with the new pedicure tools, I fixed the feet of Vito Attanasio,

In the Sixties, my sister Luisa and I went to Paris to perfect our skills at the Roger Parà's Haute Coiffure school. On top, a picture of the whole class. In the middle of the second row from bottom we are, from left: Luisa, with glasses, Roger Parà and me. Here above, one of my 'school-works': the photo of a Lido Bluebell styled by me with the teacher's guidance. On the left, again me at the graduation ceremony.

Here again, the images of the Parisian experience, so significant for our training. Above, I am sitting in the first row, third from left. Here next, a 'schoolwork' completed on another of the Lido dancers. Next to me is one of our teachers. On the side page, Roger Parà and my sister Luisa, whom he held in high esteem, photographed with the blonde Lido dancer I had also styled, here instead coiffed by my sister.

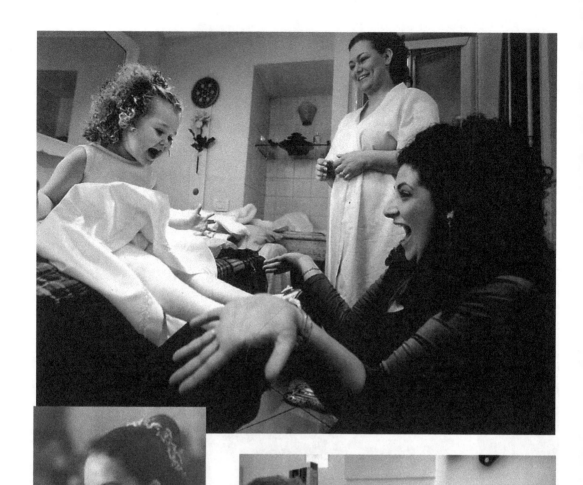

In our salon, we have always wanted to maintain a warm and friendly atmosphere, treating both the neighbour and the tourist with professionalism. That is why I never wanted to display pictures of famous clients. There were also some brides I took care of who came to offer me their bouquet after the wedding: a great emotion and gratification.

a Positanese who at the time was running the Miramare and Palazzo Murat. I was helped by Dr Giuseppe Cinque, and it was a great honour for me to have a physician as an assistant. We all called him Giovì because he grew up in America with that nickname. His brother Salvatore, on the other hand, was Salì. Their father had emigrated and taken citizenship, and his sons had also served in the military there. Back in the village, Salì had set up a boarding house near the church and his brother was precisely a doctor.

Apart from hair, I've always had an interest in foot care. The sister of our first female coworker and teacher was very talented. I learnt from her, then perfected myself – and made many people walk well. I also treated Mrs Edna Lewis, an American artist who founded the "Art Workshop Positano". They came from all over the world to learn mosaic, sculpture and painting, attracted as well by the place's beauty. For her foot problem, she also had consulted two doctors in New York, to no avail. Doctor Guido Rispoli sent her to me. It was not an easy situation, but I managed to heal her. Since then, wherever she went in the world, she would send me a postcard with kisses and greetings.

The lady owner of the Excelsior in Amalfi always arrived with a group of guests who needed our services. She only wanted to be styled by me, but she would also come for Maria Lampo's boutique, famous for her beautiful patterns. Exclusive fabrics that made the history of Positano fashion. Maria got her name from the pants, though. To the first clients, who wanted them tailored, she would reply: "I'll make them in a flash! You go for a swim and when you come back, they're ready". And so her real last name, Di Gennaro, became *Lampo*, flash, for everyone.

Meanwhile, the various activities thrived. The Buca di Bacco was increasingly becoming a gathering place for everyone, foreigners and Italians. Giulio Rispoli, my mother's cousin, was the one who took care of the image, his German wife spoke many languages and was in charge of receiving the guests. Giulio's siblings, Maria and Giuseppe, worked the first in the kitchen, the second at the bar. At the Savoia instead there was Vito D'Aiello, who had learnt English and welcomed the guests with his brother Raffaele. At the Miramare there was Carlino Cinque, at the Montemare Vito Cannavacciuolo, 'The Captain'. All self-taught tour operators, but with pleasantness, a big heart and the goodwill to go ahead. The Savino brothers built the Covo dei Saraceni and has been a success to this day. At the Marincanto there was Mrs Celeste Vespoli, who made yoghurt panettone for the guests every morning, a recipe I still use nowadays.

The Villafranca Hotel, then: it is at the top of the village's pyramid of buildings and has a magnificent view. Franca and Mario Russo have been excellent hosts. And the Poseidon, with the class of Mrs Liliana Aonzo.

At the Sponda there was the Alcione, owned by Marquis Renato Camera D'Afflitto. Great fisherman, he also had an antique shop going down to the Buca. We sold him our grandmother's antique cradle. The Agavi and the Royal came later. But they were all open from New Year's Eve to Christmas, always.

The American artist Edna Lewis founded here the "Art Workshop Positano". They came from all over the world to learn mosaic, sculpture and painting, also attracted by the beauty of the place. In the picture at the top, she is in the centre, wearing a beautiful necklace, on a visit to the village school. Above and alongside Maria '*Lampo*', whose original fabrics and talent have attracted customers from all the Coast.

The Sirenuse inaugurated in 1951. It was the large and beautiful seaside residence of the Sersale family, a veritable palace, which the four siblings decided to open up to a high-end tourism. For the launch they invited, among others, also Queen Soraya of Persia. All the newspapers talked about it and Paolo Sersale managed to have a giant picture of Positano displayed in the New York airport: the Americans fell in love with it. Then, over the years, important invitations were repeated, as in 1954 when the French Prime Minister, Pierre Mendès France, came to them.

Along with hotel owners and tour operators, the population and employees contributed from first to last to make this place one of the most beautiful and welcoming in the world. Many activities developed gradually, especially at the beach, such as the Vischitiello establishment, which later became Filiberto. In the beginning, there were still fishermen who also served as boatmen. And there was the Lucibello family, who took tourists to the little coves on the coast: the trend was full sunbathing, they were all after secluded places. Teresa Lucibello, especially, knew how to be loved. Polite, precise, she never forgot to send a boat to retrieve the clients left in the morning at the various little beaches. The Savino, on the other hand, had the first big boats and took tourists to places like Capri, Ischia and Amalfi. At the other *marina*, at Fornillo, there was Pupetto, which step by step became a beach complex with restaurant and hotel. It would be long to list all the activities of that time, establishments, restaurants, car rentals. And the buggies, waiting in front of the current pharmacy in viale Pasitea. Valentino, Pantalione, Barilotto and Peppino carried them. It was very pleasant to go around the village, imagine, slowly slowly, in a baggie. Traffic wasn't like it is now.

Coming back to us, you can say that we have experienced special moments, we have been very lucky. We had Paola of Liège – beautiful, young, with fantastic hair tossed on to one side. She would look into the salon to check if any of her girlfriends were there, or to do a styling or anything else herself. Positano was full of well-known people, but life was simple, they yearned to put on leather sandals with shorts and sit on the lion's staircase. And in the evening add a sailor sweater, if needed.

When I used to go down to our beach salon, I would walk past Anna Caldiero's one, a beautiful and good lady who had the intuition to use the knitting machine to make sweaters and invented exactly the first *marinara*, the sailor sweater, blue or with blue and white stripes, for the speedboats and yachts clientele. A beginning of Positano fashion.

The back-and-forth movement of the knitting machine could be heard from outside, always in motion. A bit further on, in the small square, there was 'Mastro Nicola': the artisan Nicola Mascolo made the first flat leather sandals with strips, fresh and, to the delight of Mayor Sersale, lightweight. To make ours an oasis of peace, the mayor didn't like clogs being sold: they made too much noise, especially going downhill. Paolo used to go to see 'Mastro Nicola' at the shop, to follow the work and make some suggestions. I don't know if this trend started in Capri or Positano,

The Sirenuse, at the top, inaugurated in 1951. There were many important invitations, which were repeated over the years, such that of the French Prime Minister Pierre Mendès France, opposite here walking in the village with his wife. At the *marina* meanwhile, Teresa Lucibello, above, never forgot to send a boat for the clients left in the morning at the little beaches. Then there were those who took the speedboat, for trips even to Capri or Ischia.

like so many other things. For example, there are the so-called *alla caprese* trousers, capri style pants, which however were once called *alla pescatora*, fishermen pants, and which Maria 'Lampo' began to make, I think first, for her female clients. They became *alla caprese* only later. When having lost the leadership of Mayor Sersale, on sandals as on much else, the village took a different direction.

At the time, if there was great looseness in clothing during the day, in the evening, thanks mainly to the Buca, but also to the parties in the villas, the ladies transformed. It was a défilé of beautiful dresses and hairstyles. And we would work late: a big sacrifice, because we had a full day behind us. It wasn't easy to keep more shops open, but we had a good team of sixteen people. Two British, one Austrian, some from Naples, Salerno, Rome, and of course the local girls who, starting from the most elementary basics, became the best with practice. Our clients were happy with us and with them, and showed it generously. If you like people, I think, whatever work you do with passion and intelligence, you do well.

Guests came every year and were wonderful encounters. With the war, we had known the precariousness of life. Seeing each other again was a victory: "We're fine, we're back". Back for the food, the sun, the sea, the welcome – and love. Yes, love! Many girls from all over the world stayed with us, married in Positano. Brides, so many we prepared! Hundreds of them. Once a young Japanese girl was coming down from the Sirenuse by the small stairway where our salon was, and she had hanging on her arm a straw bag from which white calla lilies were coming out. I was coming up from down, she smiled at me, bowed her head, and gave me in gratitude the flowers with which she married the day before, after having her hair styled by us. Unforgettable.

"Luisa and Flavia" was our trademark, with the names of us two sisters. Luisa was older than me and very good with hairdo, cutting and colour. I loved doing high hairstyles, manicure and as I said pedicure. We also had two makeup artists: Pablo Zappi Manzoni and Christian. Then my daughter Patrizia attended a good makeup school. And the results could be seen. But I never wanted to show off the pictures of the well-known personalities who came to us, as other shops did. I think clients are all equally important, from the simplest to the finest.

If brides were local, we would go to their homes and leave them free only when they were perfect. The same applies to foreigners or clients from other parts of Italy. We would go to the hotel or in a villa. Sometimes they would come back to greet us with their children, and it was a joy to see each other again.

Maestro Franco Zeffirelli, who would come from his beautiful estate by boat, would have his hair cut by my sister. Guests at his villa, many actors would come, such as Laurence Olivier, Errol Flynn, Liza Minnelli, Liz Taylor. But they also came from Amalfi, from Sorrento, from all over the Coast. To the village came Nureyev, the Russian dancer who then bought the island of Li Galli from the heirs of Léonide Massine, also a dancer, and a choreographer, with a celebrated international career

Mayor Paolo Sersale didn't like clogs being sold, they made too much noise. Instead, he loved the sandals made by Nicola Mascolo, known as 'Mastro Nicola'. Soles and strips of leather which the mayor went to see being made, to make some suggestions. The two are together in these photos. To the side, again the mayor, in front of the Town Hall with don Saverio Cinque and on the left a Positanese.

Even if I wasn't travelling to know the world, it was the world that came to us. Above, Rudolf Nureyev heads with friends to the Galli, where he lived. On his right, in the flowery dress, is Virginia Attanasio, daughter of Vito and niece of Carlino Cinque, for whom she already ran the Hotel San Pietro. Here on the right, the Quick Silver, where also happened that Sting was the disc jockey. In the centre of the photo is Pepito, one of the owners. Opposite page, director Franco Zeffirelli with Carla Fracci and, above, with Paolo Sersale during a ceremony in the church of Santa Maria Assunta.

started from the moscovite "Ballets Russes" and passed through all the most important theatres in the world. Massine had a special bond with Italy – and with Positano. Two of his three children, Lorca and Tanja, grew up with the local young people. For *Ferragosto*, the mid-August Italian holiday, the village's cinema was showing, free of charge, *Carosello Napoletano* by Ettore Giannini, in which Massine plays Pulcinella.

We have always had a great deal to do, in the summer, both for the "Moda Mare Positano" events and precisely for "Positano premia la danza - Léonide Massine". And of course, in more recent years, for "Mare, sole e cultura", the literary event conceived and wanted by Salvatore and Virginia Attanasio at Palazzo Murat, which is now held in various hotels, always with excellent authors and a large audience.

But going back to the past, there were also many British people who stayed in the winter, thanks to the dry climate. Every year, some of the ladies-in-waiting of Queen Elizabeth came to the Miramare. We learnt English from them, French at school, but not as well as English, which then gives you the chance to talk to everyone, wherever they come from. Lady Ann, beautiful and very elegant, we knew her as a client and then as Paolo Sersale's companion. They had two daughters, Marina and Giulia, who now take care of the hotel along with Franco's son, Antonio, his wife Carla and their children. Franco's wife, Carol, was also British. As a matter of fact, the beauty and magic of this place have struck a chord with many women from all over the world. Moreover, there is the class and charm of the Italian man, I think.

Once an Indian princess came to the Miramare, with a Swiss companion, and wanted us to serve her in the room. She asked me the wax depilation everywhere, even around her breasts. I remember the embarrassment, I was a girl, these were new things for us. But, slowly slowly, we got documented and always tried to provide a good service. The princess was very demanding, yet also very generous. The array of jewels scattered around her room was truly astounding. At one point, she had lost a ring and accused my sister Luisa of having stolen it, then of course she found it again, she had left it who knows where.

Another time, a German actress who was shooting a movie here, forgot her handbag, with money and jewellery, in my father's cab. They were amazed: the bag was brought back and no compensation was accepted.

The population of Positano has always been very honest, at that time the doors of the houses could be left open. Likewise, the Sirenuse left everything open, children who knew the shortcut passed by their internal stairs to get up and down the beach.

Meanwhile, being always at work, we made friends in our coiffeur, which turned into a living room. Tea with lemon granita refreshed us, it had become a ritual. The foreigners, specifically the British ladies, were always on time when they made an appointment, the Italians a little less. One group in particular: the canasta regulars, who gathered at the Buca in the afternoon and then came to us very late. They were also in a hurry, and some would even shampooing the others to help us. When they

Franca Valeri and to her right husband Vittorio Caprioli during the shooting of *Leoni al sole*. Above, another moment of filming

shot *Leoni al sole*, the 1961 film by Vittorio Caprioli, all the actors and actresses came to us. Seeing that they were egregiously attended to, the coiffeur team that had arrived from Rome was sent away. Franca Valeri, the main character, would pop up in the salon almost every day and ask about me: "Where is my girl?". Because it was me that could iron the unruly lock on her forehead just right.

Anyhow, aside from movie sets, ours was a place to be experienced, not to take a souvenir photo and go. Fireworks for celebrations, the landing of the Saracens, concerts at *Chiesa Madre*, events such as the Massine's. One year it was Maestro Zeffirelli who designed the sets for the Fornillo beach and the *marina grande*. The dance of the knights of *Romeo and Juliet*, being the stage in front of the sea rocks and the Clavel tower, with the moon behind it providing the backdrop, is a dream that I still have in my eyes. Any show taking place in this village, however, acquires an indescribable enchantment.

For the *Sbarco dei Saraceni* on *Ferragosto*, preparations began two or three months earlier. There were stage costumes, the pirate boats, which had to be discerned from those of Christians. Many boys who had come on holiday participated in the mock fighting. Positano was in complete darkness, spotlights brought from San Carlo theatre in Naples illuminated the sea in front of the *marina grande*, where the battle was taking place. On the pier they built a wood and straw church that was being set on fire, the spotlights were also illuminating the soldiers on the roofs of the houses and terraces, it really looked like the Saracens were conquering the village and that everything was burning. A movie scenario, unbelievable, in a natural amphitheatre. Then, on New Year's Eve, there was the show of fireworks over the sea.

At our salon, for Christmas, came *zeppole* and other pastries from some affectionate client. Mrs Trude Zeiss used to bring us biscuits that she had made by her Raffilina German-style: sugar-frosted saplings and stars. Thanks to one of our pupils, we would make coffee with Moka, and the foam on the side. It was a delight. Furthermore, Mrs Vivina Theodoli Valli, a very elegant client and friend, used to give a little present to all our collaborators.

My son Antonello Della Mura, who studied at Central Saint Martins College in London and at Fashion Institute Marangoni in Milan, ran a fashion boutique under his own name here in the village for twenty years. He too has been surrounded by affection, in his initiative. For example Isabella Quarantotti, Eduardo De Filippo's wife, every time she met him, wanted to know about the boutique, like a real friend. We lived as if we were one family: Luca De Filippo grew up in Positano, where he met his first partner and brought his children every year. Unfortunately, he was not as long-lived as his father, who spent his last days right at the Hotel San Pietro.

Antonello also became friends with Sydney Finch, who oversees public relations at Dior and is married to Charles Finch, son of the actor Peter. Once we invited them for dinner at my house and that's how I learnt that the mother came to the Miramare, she was my client. He remains fond of us, and keeps returning. Sidney also brought

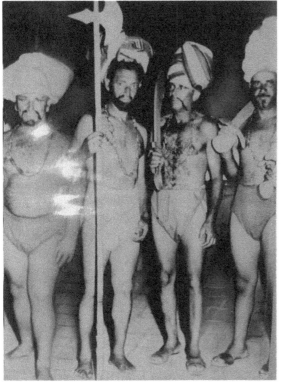

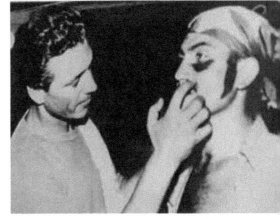

For the *Sbarco dei Saraceni* of **Ferragosto**, spotlights arrived from San Carlo theatre in Naples and illuminated the sea and houses. On the pier a wood and straw church was being set on fire, soldiers were on the roofs and terraces fighting. It really looked like the Saracens were conquering the village. A movie scenario, unbelievable. Here in the photos the preparations. Above, the choreographer and dancer Léonide Massine, who had a special bond with Positano, while following the exercises of his pupils at the Galli, where he lived.

Sharon Stone to our salon, a beautiful woman, sociable, without any haughtiness, very friendly. My son accompanied her around, and it has remained a good memory, she was enthusiastic about the place.

But a significant presence is the Gaetani family, who have always been here. The maternal grandfather, Pattison, had naval and railway industries in Naples. Here, a century ago now, he bought various houses and the Sponda tower. I styled his wife, Luisa Straub, his daughter Nora, who married Count Roberto Gaetani, and their daughters Fausta and Raimonda. Then came great-granddaughter Luisa, daughter of Fausta and friend of my daughter Patrizia. It was Patrizia who did the haircutting for Raimonda, who has become a famous international costume and set designer. I, on the other hand, took care of her feet.

The names are many, each with its own story. Mrs Ratti, from Naples, helped us a lot in forming our Municipal Library. Her daughter Francesca, who was Deputy Secretary General of the European Parliament, came to us too. From Rome, there was Mrs Milaide Riccio. Her husband Tullio was Deputy Director General of the Bank of Italy, the Italian central bank. They came for years, with their daughters Bianchina and Nicoletta, renting a beautiful house just above the Sirenuse, from Admiral Paolo Aloisi. Bianchina came back to visit us with her daughter Alessandra Baduel, a journalist, as long as her health permitted it. Mrs Milaide was a close friend of Mrs Trude, who was German but partner of the Neapolitan Dino Eminente, Honorary Consul of Iceland and producer of seafood preserves – they called him 'the king of the cod'. They too had a home up at the top of the Sponda. During the war Trude was in Rome and by exposing herself to the Germans she knew, succeeded in saving her partner, of Jewish descent, and other people, including precisely Milaide, who ended up in the prison ruled by the SS in via Tasso because she was helping the Navy's resistance. Then Trude was also deported, but was able to escape.

Apart from her biscuits, she was good with us from the beginning. We were so simple, let's just say naïve, two little girls: we were ashamed to take money.

At the closing moment, when the clients wanted to pay us, Luisa and I blushed and ran away, sometimes both of us together. We would find ourselves confused shoulder to shoulder, jammed in the small door leading into the house, wondering what to do with each other. It was Mrs Zeiss who gave us our first lesson on the subject: "You work and it is not a game, you have to get used to the fact that money is what you deserve!". With patience, she scolded us affectionately. And we got used to it. Said today, it may sound a presumption. But if I write it, it is to try to convey the atmosphere of the time, at least in our family. Two home-raised girls like my sister and I, not even in our twenties, we didn't handle money that much. Mum, as long as she was there, had some small properties she rented out. Our father had the shop, indeed, but we didn't have to deal with. A traditional family. We were not exposed to any direct contact with customers. So, when sadly mom succumbed to the disease, it also occurred that her brother was able to take over all the inheritance.

Here above Lietta Scialoja Camicia. Such a dear client and friend, she directed me to Paris for my husband's treatments. She herself had been operated on several times and sent me to her doctor, Professor Jacques Reynier, at the Clinique de Passy. Left, a foreign vacationer receiving his mail.

At that point, the idea of a lady's hairdresser, from a passion and pursuit of satisfaction that was, became a real necessity. And perhaps, that was precisely why Luisa and I were ashamed, at first. Nonetheless, then we learnt and quickly, but always trying to preserve our own way of welcoming clients: a homelike atmosphere, professional and affectionate at the same time.

Even certain minor complications, we solved them in our way. One, for example, was represented by Mrs Coltellacci's many beautiful and precious rings. A very good client of ours, she frequented the beach salon. She arrived from the Covo dei Saraceni, always with her umbrella open, to shield herself from the sun – a rarity, in those days, a woman who didn't like tanning – and always with her hands laden with these beautiful rings. As soon as she sat down, she would take them off and scatter them on the shelf. To avoid any risk, my sister would arrive and slip them all on her fingers.

Perhaps this warm atmosphere also made certain of our clients want to protect us. In 1976 my husband Michele had a cancer and metastasis had formed near an important vein: they had given me no hope, in Rome. I was helped by another very dear client and friend, Lietta Scialoja Camicia, who had a boutique on via Condotti in Rome. A special woman: she was volunteering at the Bambin Gesù Hospital for children. She had been operated on several times for cancer and referred me to Professor Jacques Reynier at the Clinique de Passy in Paris. And who do I meet? Mrs Riccio, who was accompanying her brother Carlo also for anticancer treatments at the same clinic. They were the ones who told me that there was a convention with the French government and accompanied me to social security. So I was able to get some refunds, it was so helpful.

In any case, after Paris, in 1977, sadly the father of my children ended suffering. I turned to our *Madonna* of Positano to help me move on. But I was lucky, because I found the affection and love of a wonderful man who was fond of me since I was a teenager. Our paths had parted then, and I did marry very young. He, on the other hand, never got married, and when he saw me left alone had the courage, with extreme delicacy, to tell me what was in his mind and heart. His name is Pasquale Collina. We have been together for more than forty years, I agreed to marry him, and we love each other as we did in the early days. It is this loving that helps me, as if was oxygen. Avoiding anger and misunderstandings is always my purpose. Thankfully, I had who could understand me. And my work, fundamental.

My clients were counsellors also with outfits, their class guided us. Mrs Pupa Zucchi from Milan, the husband had the textile factory with that name, even had custom made shoes for me, with the side strap and half heel, closed only in the front. When I would go to the Paris clinic in the morning, with Nina Ricci's foulards, the reversible Agnone wool coat and my beautiful shoes, Professor Reynier would call me *"la petite belle femme du sud d'Italie"*. If he had known Positano and those who frequented it, he would have been very surprised.

Pupa Zucchi, above with one of her two sons at sea, had even tailored shoes made for me. In the other pictures, the Riccio family at the Buca: top left Milaide, my very fond client, and friend also with Lietta and Trude. Top right, her husband Tullio with their daughter Bianchina. Next here, on the right the granddaughter Alessandra Baduel, in the centre the lawyer Vittorio Ripa di Meana and on the left his daughter Virginia.

In 1977 the father of my children was disgracefully defeated by the disease. Left alone, I had the good fortune to receive the offer to get together from a wonderful man, who loved me since I was a girl. Next here, Pasquale Collina and I on our honeymoon in Rome in 1981. Below, several years later, Pasquale receives my staff's care at the salon. I am in the centre and behind me are, from left: Tina Manzi, Azzurra Cacace, Marcellina Grotta, Anna Pica and Marcella Buonocore, while at work you see Livia Carandente.

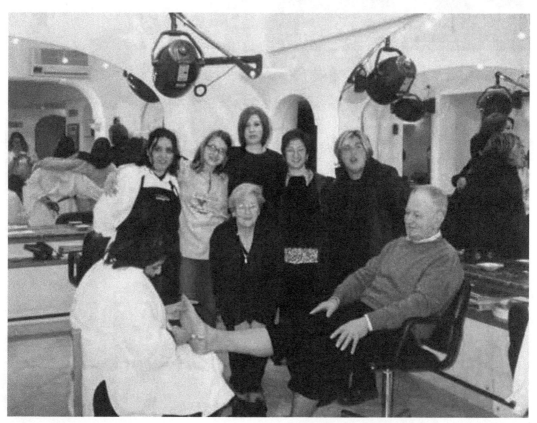

My daughter Patrizia and Alfonso Milano got married in 1994 and celebrated by sailing to Praia, the beach of Praiano. At the top, the two of them with Pasquale and I on either side, and my nephews below. From left: Luisa, Michela and Alessio. The first is my sister's granddaughter, the other two are Maria's children. Beside, there is me looking out the windows of our salon at the Mulini. Next here, the wedding of my daughter Maria with Gabriele Mandara in 1983, at the church of Santa Maria Assunta.

Then in Paris there was Mrs Olga Dax Davidoff. As soon as she knew I was there she wanted me at her house, and showed the many beautiful pictures of the trips she had taken, precisely with Carlino Cinque of the San Pietro and his companion Liliana Aonzo. She was a woman of Russian descent, and great culture. Once we went together to Vuitton, which was still on Avenue Marceau. The manager, Russian like her, looked at me a little astonished. At the time they frowned upon Italians because they had made fakes. In any case, I only bought a bag for one of my female collaborators. As for me, I didn't want it: a symbol of an ostentation, it reminded me of those girls who, eager to have certain objects, accept the courtship of men they do not love at all. I didn't like it.

Among our clients, by the way, there were even those who put us on the same level as Paris, recognizing us, in addition, an advantage: I had for several years a *Figaro* journalist who used to come to the Covo dei Saraceni. She was very happy with the way I did her blond highlights. "Flavia", she told me, "I pay for the flight and the hairstyling here with you, and it costs me less than the Carita sisters in Paris".

We had a nice international clientele for this reason, too. Fate then didn't want it, but Mrs Nancy Guggenheim, a woman of great culture, was acquainted with Alexander – at the time, one of the most famous Parisian coiffeurs – and she suggested, if I wanted, to recommend me to him, because I was good and could have a brilliant career. Another client, had three shops in London and wanted me to manage them for her, she liked the way I styled her hair. Unfortunately, I couldn't move, due to the serious health problems that I had in my family. But I have to say that now I'm so glad I stayed here, although I've now left my salon. I live in front of the sea, an immense space. The beauty of Positano is that the houses are on top of each other, so each one gets a part of the scenery. Being very characteristic, it has been portrayed by artists from all over the world. About them, Matilde Romito, a client and friend of mine who is an art expert, has published wonderful books: *Vieni qui il paese è una fiaba*, *La pittura di Positano nel '900* and many others about the Coast.

Along with art, she described the people, the migrations and the changes, which have been many, some even negative. But there was work for everyone, and the village provided employment to many people outside as well. During the Positano fashion period, it gave jobs in sewing as far as Puglia.

In our own small way, we helped too. Clients used to get touchups every fortnight, total colour once a month, manicure every week and pedicure every two weeks. Slowly slowly, the local girls and women also began to take care of their bodies. Hot wax depilation, there was nothing else and it was a little painful, but for beauty this and more. Then we began to use a very light makeup for brides. At the time, the parish priests were very strict: "Neither exaggerated necklines, nor makeup". But it was a pain to see those tense and slightly dull little faces in the photographs. And instead, after a light maquillage, we felt such a joy seeing the bride radiant, smiling and grateful.

An American girl who married here was a Protestant. To have a pastor, the wedding was celebrated in Capri, but the reception was in Positano. On the return trip, I was afraid that, with the speedboat in full swing, the wind would ruin her hairstyle. In the photos, in addition to the beautiful flowers, you can see how worried I am. I felt nauseous. But my system, with hidden hairpins and rolled locks underneath, worked.

I have always loved doing high hairstyles. And we took care of our clients both by going to hotels and their homes, or to the salon. The result was visible, and the photos show it.

One winter, American mother and daughter came from the Sirenuse, to do their hair and everything else. Pleased with the treatment, they announced that the girl was getting married here in the spring and chose us to take care of the hairstyle. They were Protestant and in order to have a pastor, the wedding was celebrated in Capri. My daughter Patrizia and I went with them to the Hotel Quisisana. The party, however, was in Positano, at the Covo dei Saraceni.

We left at seven in the morning on the bride's speedboat and returned with the guests on a large, slower boat. From there, I watched the girl moving away, standing in the speedboat, worried sick: I was afraid the wind would ruin her hairstyle! Instead everything went well, my system had worked. The bun hairstyle turned out soft, but I built it up inside with hairpins: I rolled the locks and fixed them slightly twisted. And so nothing melted away, not even in the wind of the crossing. I had become nauseous from anxiety, but I had done it. The bride and the ladies of the family had very beautiful jewels and grand luxury dresses. But I have to say that, again perhaps because of my naïveté, when I learnt that all that money came from a gun factory, I also got sick about: they were the owners of the Colt.

Then the fashion of getting married in the most beautiful places in the world broke out. And what about our whole Coast, Capri, Sorrento, Ischia – Ravello with its wonderful gardens. Women came from New Zealand, Iceland, Australia, London, Ireland, the United States, Paraguay, Ecuador – and of course Italians. Most would have their pictures taken at our small stairway in front of the salon. Plenty of times we were there all day, because in order to rent the ads would write "Positano", while possibly the houses were even 20 kilometres away. And avoiding them from going back and forth, we would host them: they would come with the dress and prepare themselves in the salon. The church of Santa Maria Assunta is a five-minute walk away. Then they would hug and thank us, because they understood that it was a special treatment.

Clearly this gave work to everyone, from the florist to the taxi drivers, the restaurants, the hotels. We all worked hard, collaborators and entrepreneurs, with impossible schedules, but we did it with pleasure because we created the future for everyone.

Thinking about the past, a very sweet memory surfaces: Mrs Della Rocca, a very fine woman, petite but of an extraordinary elegance. She had a very beautiful and huge house, so during the war they stayed here to avoid the bombing of Naples. There was the typhoid epidemic, she lost a daughter. Then, both in winter and summer, she would come to go to the cemetery. On the way down, she would stop in our salon, and I would style her hair. It was always a nice meeting. Now here is her son Carlo, who has a house at the Sponda in the Gaetani property and comes with his wife Mirella De Miro and their children. Positano, if it gets into your heart, becomes part of you.

Another fond memory is Marquise Anna Sersale, the eldest of the siblings, with her inseparable basset hounds and many friendships among nobles and princesses,

Here above Anna Sersale. The marquise was a great swimmer. On the side, Adolfo Bella, in a rowboat and on his speedboat. As a young man he had also been a partisan. At the top, you can see his restaurant at Laurito beach, towards Praiano: a big success, well-deserved and lasting over the years.

who came to visit her. When she was nearing the end Carla, Antonio's wife, called me. Anna was in bed, I did her hands and feet for the last time, it was a farewell, and we were moved. She had no children, like her brother Aldo, who always carried *le belle guaglione*, the pretty girls, on his goitre. In addition to Aldo's goitre, there were also some beautiful and very fast speedboats. Engineer De Amici, Carlino Cinque, Auricchio, Consul Eminente and the Sersale family had them: they were having fun waterskiing. Adolfo Bella and Michele Irace, instead, offered it to tourists, it was their job. There was also a group of divers, called '*i corallieri*', the coralliers, who did underwater fishing. And there was the deluxe sailing boat of the sovereigns Juliana and Bernhard of the Netherlands, who stayed at the Covo dei Saraceni. Finally, only one cutter, belonging to Guggenheim's son.

And speaking of the Sirenuse, there is to be told about Mrs Wilma Gagliardi. With her husband and the daughter Alessandra, they used to stay at the hotel for the whole summer. They were special guests, so much so that Anna Sersale allowed the little girl to organize some recitals with her peers for the clients, despite the fact that, as a rule, children were not allowed in the hotel. I would help them with hairstyling and makeup, because my son Antonello, Alessandra's best friend, would attend the small plays. It was an elegant and refined place, yes, but at the same time hospitable and almost familiar: there were precisely those who stayed for long periods as if it were their own home.

In those years, at the end of the season there was a hairstyle competition, with an award ceremony and a party. Ladies would come to us to get ready, and once Mrs Zucchi won: she had added a sprig of bougainvillaea in the elaborate chignon we had made for her. The bougainvillaea was 'the flower of Positano' for everyone and she got the prize, a beautiful foulard in the latest fashion. The Sirenuse also held the pasta party, with many different courses: short, long, with all kinds of pasta sauces and seasonings. The family invited about two hundred people.

Always at the end of the season, Carlino Cinque hosted a dinner for all the guests at his little cove. The Hotel San Pietro was his dream, at that tip of the mountain he created an original and elegant place, full of the flowers of his niece Virginia that takes care of it, together with his sons Carlo and Vito, detached from the hustle and bustle of mass tourism.

But thinking of Anna again, there is to remember her great friend: Princess Santa Borghese Hercolani. She had bought the Fornillo tower, already known by the name of its previous owner, the Swiss intellectual Gilbert Clavel, who in the early decades of the Twentieth century had rebuilt and filled it with the works of his friend Fortunato Depero. Anna and Santa were great swimmers, even when elderly by dint of armfuls they would push themselves out, the two of them alone in the middle of the sea, without any fear. The princess was not fond of dyes, she came to me only for washing and styling. She was a sensible and clever woman, a good presence for the village, and able to keep at the best that tower where so many artists have passed, from Picasso to Cocteau, to Marinetti. Helping her a lot, with passion and devotion

My son Antonello here above in his boutique, also pictured at the top. Beside, he is with Denzel Washington, habitué of Positano. As a child Antonello was close friends with Alessandra Gagliardi, nearby he is with her at the pool of the Sirenuse, where Alessandra stayed with her mother and where she was allowed to organize small children's plays for the guests. Antonello participated, so I helped them with hairstyles and makeup.

Brides, so many we prepared! Hundreds of them, both before and after the blast of the fashion to get married here. We used to care for hair and makeup, just a bit of maquillage until the parish priest was against it. But it made them radiant. We also prepared the girls as bridesmaids, or for their First Communion. Brides from outside sometimes came back to visit us with their children, and it was a joy.

to the place, there was Daniele Esposito. A Positanese from Fornillo, custodian of the tower, it was to him that Santa Hercolani left the Depero collection: she knew he would keep it entire and at its best, in fact those paintings are often on display in various museums.

Among the many who have spent plenty of time with us, summer and winter, there is the actor Peter Weller. He lived at the Sirenuse and started studying for university. Now he is married to the beautiful Shari Stowe and they bought a house here, at least once a year they come back to visit. The Fontana sisters also had a house in Positano – and they too have been in our salon. The celebrities are countless, from Carla Fracci to Angelica Ippolito, from Daria Nicolodi to Renzo Arbore, Don Lurio, Raffaella Carrà, as well as the actors Marisa Tomei and Robert Downey Junior, who shot *Only you* here, with scenes at our small stairway. Which is a constant passage of tourists. Brides taking souvenir photos, movies, TV series – it's like a *prima donna*, even ranked among the most photographed places in the world. But I remember the young scions Schisano, Perrella, Pugliese, Ammaniti, going down through the small stairway with a *cuoppo*, the basket to go fishing, on their shoulders. Together we watched them grow.

In front of us, built a beautiful house the theatre director Giorgio De Lullo, and often hosted the actors from the Piccolo of Milan, people such as Anna Maria Guarnieri or Romolo Valli. I celebrated my eighteenth birthday at the De Lullo's house: I was friends with their nephews, and they offered me the party. Roberto Murolo also came to the small stairway. Together with Nino from Positano, they sang accompanying each other on guitar, in homage to a beautiful girl named Maria, owner of the Bar Centrale in the square. The actress Andreina Pagnani, used instead to come, in the summer, to San Pietro. I still have the memory of the beautiful tone of voice she retained despite her age. When younger, she stayed in a villa at Fornillo. My father would go with his cab to pick her up in Rome, together with Alberto Sordi, her love.

And then there was our '*Ferragosto's* balcony', from where everyone wanted to face out and witness the procession. The fashion designer Giambattista Valli, dear friend of my son, was always coming up, so he could see the *Madonna* passing by a few metres away. Once, with him came Alba and Francesco Clemente, one of the most popular contemporary Italian painters. The entrepreneur Alfonso Costa, a friend of my daughter Patrizia, sometimes also came to see the *Madonna* and brought Ben Carson, who with enormous sacrifices, being of dark skin, became an excellent neurosurgeon, famous for having separated twins joined by their heads.

It's a magic evening, that one, also of good wish for the rest of the year. Yet the marching band often passed by. At every celebration in the other quarters, or in the villages of Montepertuso and Nocelle, they would come down to the *Chiesa Madre* to greet the *Madonna* and we would all go outside.

From those years, there is also something Alessandra found: an old address book that her grandmother Milaide Riccio kept here. There are so many names in it –

NOME	N.	NOME	N.
Alviži (v.e colombo 34)	75106	Bar internazionale	045
		Brunori -185	058
antifurno Finvi		Benzoni 78	1044
Punta Rejinella	75394		
		Barba Mimì (9509)	230
		Bertolè	079

Other memories were triggered by an old address book of Milaide Riccio, up here with the dachshund Teo, which has all the phone numbers of Positano in it. There are the names of that extended community that had been created between us of Positano and these early tourists. Beside Mimì Barba, at '230', at the time taxi driver, then jeweller.

and for me, new memories – of that extended community that existed between us of Positano and these early tourists. Only the last digits are almost always marked, because all the phones in the village began with a '75'. The first is that of Admiral Paolo Aloisi, their landlord, '106'. Then there's Barba Mimì, '230', at that time a taxi driver, now he has the "Da Mimì" jewellery, next to the pharmacy. And Mr and Mrs Bertolli, the oil people, '079'. They always came in my father's cab. The lady had teased me for a lifetime. One day, I was still a child, she saw me at the front door, at the small stairway: "But you are Pompeo's daughter, aren't you?". And I: "I don't know... I'll go ask mom". Mocked for years! Regarding them, I also remember the brother, who married a dancer, beautiful woman and great poise. Following is the list of hotels, from Buca to San Pietro, Covo, Poseidon, Miramare, Alcione, Ancora, Vittoria, Sirenuse, Savoia, Marincanto, up to the Primavera boarding house, just below the Sirenuse, which is no longer there. And then the Caròla, '941', a family that took a house near the church, the California, '382', a residence that rented out apartments here at the Sponda. Mrs Nicolini lived there. She had a little shop with antiques at the small arch of the beach, and always reminded everyone that she was relative of Pope Roncalli, Giovanni XXIII. Great lady, indeed, very respectable but she needed to earn. From Rome, she had moved here, in the residence. At that time, rents could even be annual and weren't too expensive. Rather, they just had to hope that someone would take a house for all the twelve months. Then there is Caporale, '374', the restaurant where the good cooking was entrusted to the wife Maria, who had invented the *Caporalessa*, a baked red sauce pasta, with fried eggplants, capers and olives, mixed with fior di latte and pecorino cheese. And there is Countess Laura Carafa, '409' the number.

Neapolitan noblewoman from a high-ranking family, who moved to Positano in the postwar period: unfortunately, she had lost all her possessions.

In the mid-Fifties, therefore, she decided to open a small boutique near piazza dei Mulini, next to where the cinema was at the time. She had an excellent worker, Florinda Ferrero – and obviously, a very good taste. The ladies all got their clothes from her, partly also to help. The clothes were made from the most varied materials. Florinda and the countess had imagination and also used fabrics from curtains and bedspreads that they transformed into beautiful dresses. But in Positano the real age of tourism had not yet begun, there wasn't much profit. Plus, regrettably, the countess was not really used to handling money. She didn't know how to do the math. So, like everyone else, she committed to suppliers to pay for the fabrics at the end of the season, the new ones and not the ones retrieved from curtains, of course. But then, when she sold a dress, she calculated it as a net profit and spent it, without keeping the share to pay for the materials: she was constantly in the red. At lunchtime, during the closure of the atelier, she often came to do a hairstyling. We still had only one coiffeur room at the small stairway. Beyond that room was our house: we always invited her to the table. She taught us a lot about manicuring.

NOME	N.	NOME	N.
Alberghi:		Vittoria	875049
Firenze	875055		
Buca	006	Primavera	016
Miramare	022		
Alcione 198	052	Marincanto	130
Ancora	318		
Pensione	014		
Savino	003		
Coro	059		
Confino S. Pietro	75455		

NOME	N.	NOME	N.
~~Confino~~	~~068~~	De Amicis	095
Carola	341	D'Urso 41	820
			821
Cinema	047	Dorothy	538
Carad	409	Del Pesco	286
California	382		
Caporale	374		

C
E
G
I
L
N
P

Carlino Cinque, on the side with his niece Virginia Attanasio and on top with his boxer Betty, had done so much for Positano. The Hotel San Pietro was his dream, at that tip of the mountain he created an original and elegant place. Before he was at the Miramare, at the '022'. The village phone numbers all began with a '75' and you didn't need to write that down, you just mark the last three digits.

No metal tools, just rosewood sticks: the ones still in use today. She also introduced us to Likeria, a magnificent nail cream which at that time was only produced in France. We constantly followed all the good advice. Thirsty for knowledge, we learnt day by day with passion.

At 'D' is De Amici, '095' – and what memories. The engineer Vittorio De Amici, who worked with Astaldi, built the first airport in the Belgian Congo with the British. A house in Kenya and Congo, a villa in Rome and Positano. His wife was a very dear client of mine and gave me several jewels – later all stolen, unfortunately. She would come especially from Rome to get hair, manicure and pedicure, always on Sundays: we would open for her. Very close to where I live now, a little outside, at the top of the Sponda, villa De Amici is now a small hotel, La Fenice, in a strategic location, in front of the former villa Zeffirelli, with a descent to the sea and a small beach. The owner is the mother of Gabriele, husband of my daughter Maria. Years ago, they also had Chancellor Gerhard Schröder as a guest, enthusiastic about the Coast and preceded by a team of agents who came a month earlier to wire the whole area.

In the long period of the war ending, just up to the liberation of Northern Italy, the De Amici hosted General Clark, the man of the Salerno Landings. The Anglo-American command had set up at Bruno's bar, not far away, and the general stayed at villa De Amici until the Allies were in Italy. At that time we, on the other hand, had Tommy and Jimmy as guests. Tommy soldier, Jimmy officer. Mom rented them two rooms on via Monte, towards Punta Reginella, where we had a beautiful villa with a garden. At Christmas time, Tommy and Jimmy returned from a trip to Naples with presents. For me, the tiny shepherds and camels of the crib, for my sister Luisa the book *One Thousand and One Nights*, with the illustrations, wonderful.

I don't even know how many people in the village borrowed it. It was a total novelty for Positano. I was very fond of reading, and in the little street below our small stairway used to come a retired teacher who sold children's books. Since during the winter we let him lay both the books and the display, he would lend me volumes in return, which I would devour in no time. And my mother also bought me some, to help him. She also had the habit of the three bowls by the fireplace. Every day she would put at heat on the fireplace three dishes of pasta and beans or whatever she cooked: after lunch, her protégés, elderly people in need, would appear, and she would put their plate and a glass of wine on a small table at the entrance.

Still at 'D', there is '71-820': it indicates the D'Urso family, father and son, who had a villa in Conca dei Marini, just before Amalfi. Mario, the senator, is all too well-known for I to be the one to remind who he was. A Neapolitan who grew up in America and lived between business and 'dolce vita', then a movie in which for fun he also starred. He always came to Positano. The seaside villa had been bought by his father, lawyer Sandro D'Urso, and had been restored by a leading Spanish architect, Julio Lafuente. Prince Riccardo di Sangro had previously lived there. It was he, in the postwar period, who had what was a *tonnara* for fishermen transformed

In the postwar period, there were not many hotels: the Margherita, the Roma, the Savoia, the Miramare, the Maresca, the Montemare, the Villafranca. Beside, the family of the owners in front of the Savoia. From left, Carolina, Maria, Raffaele and Vito D'Aiello, very close to Marquise de Ruggiero.

by Coco Chanel, who designed the ceramics for all the coverings. To the D'Urso went Jackie Kennedy, lawyer Agnelli, the Queen of the Netherlands. It was the Sixties, then the villa was sold to the Moët et Chandon champagne owner, and it became villa Chandon. And just to remember our love for cooking as well, I would add that Prince of Sirignano, known as '*Pupetto*', while being a guest of the D'Urso family invented *spaghetti alla Nerano*, with fried zucchini and provolone cheese, which are still eaten. Even from the D'Urso's house, they all ended up at ours, for the evenings at the Buca. It was Sandro, the dad lawyer, who had Princess Margaret of England come for dinner at the Sirenuse. And from the Sirenuse, her lady-in-waiting came down to do the hairstyle by "Luisa and Flavia".

Eva, '032', is Marquise Eva de Ruggiero, cousin of the Sersale family. She opened the famous first boutique in Positano, preceding also that of Countess Carafa, in the early Fifties. She sewed to measure with the seamstress. In 1958, to celebrate my 18th birthday, she had a very beautiful dress tailored for me, balloon style and using Ken Scott fabrics with a lovely flower pattern. It was all the rage. For some years it was the only shop where one could buy nice clothes. The marquise was friends with the Fontana sisters and here in Positano they lived nearby, at the small staircase leading to the Miramare. She lived permanently in the village and had a relationship, then called 'affectionate friendship', with Vito of the Hotel Savoia. They never married, however they loved each other very much. The only thing the marquise complained about was the lack of travels. Vito was always working, while she would have loved so much to move around.

It was still Eva who made me the suit when I got married in 1961. Not the wedding dress, which I bought in a dedicated atelier in Salerno, but the travel outfit: jacket, dress, and overcoat. With those, I went to Rome, Milan, Venice, Assisi. Yes, the overcoat, because it was January. Here in Positano, we do everything in winter. Meetings, family parties, ceremonies, to avoid overlapping with summer work: in those months, there is not even time to scratch your head! When my sister Luisa got married, three years before me, she too had Eva's travel outfit. But besides the boutiques, in those years there were many other initiatives. There was Mrs Kovalisca, who devoted herself to pottery. It was she that invented the little donkeys with side wicker baskets, now on sale throughout the village, and began to dye fabrics, while Raffaella Durso, known as '*Filuccia*', made the first espadrillas, very simple, with twine and cloth.

At 'F', there is us, '447' the salon and '317' the house – the first is still the same, never changed. At 'G' there is Gargiulo home appliances, '060'. He sold washing machines, cookers, stoves, TVs, and was the one to bring the gas cylinders for kitchens to the houses. The store was at Chiesa Nuova, now gone. He married very late and had an only daughter, beautiful and with a wonderful voice. Gasser, '088', was an elderly German lady who had a villa in Fornillo, and often stayed here even in the winter. Of course, she would come to me. She had extremely thin hair, white, we dyed it blonde. Nora Gaetani, '155', is Raimonda and Fausta's mother.

It was the Knight, in the address book '078', at the time jewellers in Naples and very fond of the village, who helped don Raffaele when it was needed to redo the crown of our statue of the *Madonna* with the green mantle. It was stolen, and everyone contributed to the expense. Fabrizio Knight, up here in the boat, brought the gold collected to a trusted goldsmith and contributed himself.

At 'I', are the *idraulici*, the plumbers. Gigino, '154', was Luigi Paone, a Neapolitan married here, now there is his grandson. Next is the pipefitter's number, Nicola Talamo, also a plumber, '472'. For the Positano of the Fifties and Sixties, two plumbers were the minimum: just think about all the needs of the hotels. And then boarding houses were opening, villas were renovating: everyone was doing new bathrooms. There was a lot of work. At ours the first sink was put up by Gigino, in fact. It was the end of 1956, I still remember it. Before, we had to manage with plastic headrests that ended in funnels: underneath we would place a tub and wash with the water jug.

The Knight, '078', at the time jewellers in Naples, with a shop near piazza dei Martiri, are a family with close ties to the village. They were the ones who helped the parish priest, don Raffaele Talamo, to redo the crown of our beautiful statue of the *Madonna Assunta*, which we have in the central church. Thieves had stolen it. At that point, all Positano donated gold – some more and some less depending on the possibilities, of course. We are very fond of our *Madonna* with the green mantle and the child in her arms. It was created so as not to move the ancient icon of the *Madonna Nera*, Black Madonna, from the altar and instead be able to have a statue to carry in procession. That, too, has its own story, that is say legend, according to which it was given to the Positanesi by the sailors of a vessel that came from the East, and ended up in dead calm in front of the village. In order to move, the crew began to unload weight. In particular, though, there was a wrapper, a bale of silk, that 'spoke'. And it kept repeating: "*Posa, posa*", lay, lay. Lay me here, the sailors understood.

And so they did, taking the wrapper to the beach and immediately after succeeding to set sail into the sea. In that bale of silk was the icon of the *Madonna Nera*, for which the church and monastery were erected near the *Marina*. But it was too precious to carry in procession. So now, for us the statue that replaces it is more important. At the time of the theft and the donations, therefore, it was Fabrizio Knight who helped don Raffaele Talamo, bringing the gold collected to a trusted goldsmith in Naples to redo the crown, and also contributing financially himself. A nice person, a splendid couple with his wife born Ruffo di Calabria, friend of Paola of Liége. Fabrizio's brother, Carlo, wrote a beautiful book on Positano and Capri at the beginning of the Twentieth century, *La Torre di Clavel*, about the tower now in custody of Daniele Esposito.

Casa Scielzo is at '173'. Again, it is certainly not up to me to recall the figure of Roberto Scielzo. He was an artist who also worked for the Rome Opera House. Here he left many traces of his work as a painter, architect and stage designer. His are the decorations of various places, such as the Hotel Eden Rock, which at the restaurant Adamo ed Eva exhibits his *Earthly Paradise* ceramic. His was the idea of making the little gates with horizontal bars so as not to 'disturb' with the vertical ones the vision of the panorama, his were the set designs for the historical parade in Amalfi and for the famous *Sbarco dei Saraceni* that I have already remembered. Conceived

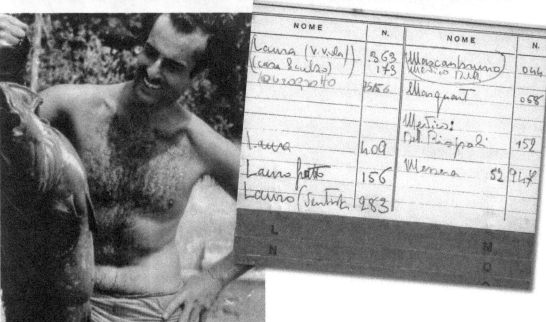

The dentist Lauro was also a good fisherman.
Above Daniele Esposito, still a boy with Princess
Santa Borghese Hercolani on a boat, near the
Clavel Tower where she lived and where Daniele
was, and remained, the passionate keeper.

Positano - Panorama

Those were years when they refurbished houses and the village. Beside, works at the pier. Above a vintage postcard. On the next page, in the foreground the Trasita Tower, readapted by Marquis Giorgio Gozzi, a diplomat. The wife had a dog considered as a child: when she came, we had to put a towel on an armchair to accommodate him. Now the tower, with Marina and Roberto Parlato's good taste, has become a wonderful suite. Behind is Clavel Tower, where Depero, Picasso and Cocteau passed by.

by Admiral Aloisi and sought by Mayor Sersale, in the Fifties every August the 14th saw the whole village stage the landing on the beach, once even with a giant wooden elephant ridden by the admiral himself. Among other things, Scielzo did the Zagara, the homonymous bar under the small stairway in front of our salon. *Zagara* is the blossom of lemon and orange trees, and he drew the bas-relief that is outside, just with the yellow-coloured flower. And his also are the primary schools: on each floor, there are bas-reliefs on the walls, small decorations designed by Scielzo. It was Paolo Sersale who as mayor gave him the assignments. He lived in Palazzo Perrella, near the Eden Rock, on the street that comes back after the Sponda and then goes up around the village.

Antonella Lauro Grotto, '156', was the wife of a medicine representative of the Carlo Erba. She was very nice, classic Neapolitan. In *Leoni al sole* she participates in a scene with other ladies who pretend to play cards, and even says a movie line. At the salon, she came mocking us: "So, girls, now now, right away, come on, come on!". She was very fond of us.

Of the dentist Lauro, at '283', unfortunately I don't remember the name, but the one of his son Skipper I do. His father was handsome. Even a playboy when he was young, he was always at the Buca. He married an American journalist, and they had Skipper, who grew up here happily. Sadly, he died at the age of 12, up in the mountains, because of a breathing crisis. It was the early Seventies, I knew all those kids, they would pass under the salon windows coming and going from the sea and games.

Thursdays, for example, were a special day for them. There was the new film coming by minivan, from Sorrento I think: everyone inside the theatre next to our salon, to see cowboys, Indians, gun fights, martians on earth. Things like that, typical of movies of the time. On the way out, endless shouts, fake shootings between improvised cowboys, and then they would move a few meters, to the Quick Silver, in the Valle dei Mulini, where now there is a huge parking lot. Too bad to do that they also destroyed the garden, with a centuries-old walnut tree, the fountain with the stone tub where the women used to go to wash, all that greenery for those who wanted to stay in the cool for a while.

The nightclub was born in the late Sixties and on Thursday afternoons it opened to young boys and girls, who certainly couldn't be allowed to go to the *soirées*. A few 100 liras for a sandwich, Coca Cola and entrance, so they had fun after the movie, with a snack included, until it was time to go home for dinner. Later, the adult evening would begin, like every day of the summer season. Anything happened, even Sting being the disc jockey. It was him, during a visit in the Eighties, now famous, who recalled that to one of the Quick Silver's owners, Pepito of the dress shop. Sting had come to look for a house, seeing villa Tre Ville and villa Nuvolari. He had almost made up his mind, but then the traffic discouraged him, I believe. At least that's what is said: he got stuck in a traffic jam, got angry and changed his

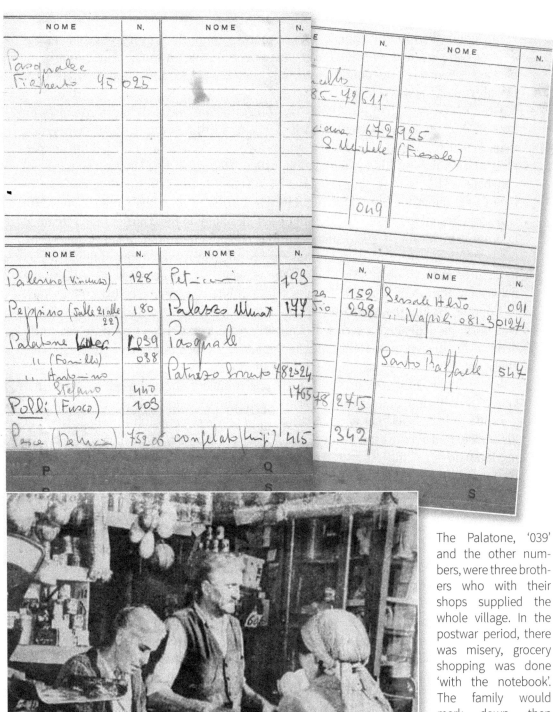

NOME	N.	NOME	N.
Pasquale e Fi_berto	45 025		

NOME	N.
_elts 85 - 42	611
_iana S. M_chele (Fiesole)	672 925
	049

NOME	N.	NOME	N.
Palesino (Vincenzo)	128	Pet_icc_	199
Peppino (dalle 21 alle 22)	180	Palazzo Murat	144
Palatone ~~Killer~~	039	Pasquale	
" (Famiglia)	038	Patrizzo Sorrento	482524
" Anto_ino Stefano	440		176548
Polli (Fusco)	103		
Pesce (Delicia)	75206	confelato (Lui_')	415

N.	NOME	N.
152	Sensale Nevo	091
238	" Napoli 081-3	01271
275	Santo Raffaele	544
342		

The Palatone, '039' and the other numbers, were three brothers who with their shops supplied the whole village. In the postwar period, there was misery, grocery shopping was done 'with the notebook'. The family would mark down, then when the time came to slaughter and sell the calf raised in the mountain, they would pay the debt, at least in part.

mind, going then to buy it in Tuscany. Apart from tourists, every family here has at least two cars, and unfortunately when Paolo Sersale was mayor his proposal of parking lots only at the entrances of the village, with the provision of small cars, possibly electric, was rejected.

Bruno Marquardt had the '058'. My son Antonello was very close friends with his son Alberto, who sadly died early. He was a brilliant and party-loving young man. When Antonello worked in the film industry, Alberto also hosted him in Naples, in the palace of his mother Emilia, called '*Pupa*', of the Dukes of Tuttavilla di Calabritto. The palace is in piazza dei Martiri and it was precisely the collapse of a part of it under the bombings that brought Emilia to meet the painter Bruno. He had already settled in Positano, fleeing Nazi Germany in the Thirties, and remained here until his death in 1981, marrying that Neapolitan noblewoman displaced by the bombings. Marquardt was famous for his underwater passion and the artworks he painted even while at sea, being in the water. His subjects were the village, the fishermen, the boats, the small coves. He exhibited everywhere, from New York to London, Berlin, the Venice Biennale. But he never left Positano. When Alberto was born, he dedicated a series of paintings to him: the story of a little sea turtle discovering the world. A gentle and good man. The wife came to me, obviously, like everyone. Always in pants, she wore nice short hair.

Pasquale and Filiberto, at '025', were one lifeguard and the other owner of the bathing establishment next to the Caravella, the first one to build concrete cabins.

Filiberto had a German wife, Adelina, who had a sweet tooth for chocolate, but hid it from him. At the grocery store, Adelina asked for the bar and then said: "Please mark potatoes". Childless, she left everything to the relatives of the Hotel Savoia. Raffaele, Filiberto's cousin, had also married a German, Regina. We have welcomed many foreigners here, not only Americans or English but precisely many Germans, and Swiss, Scottish, Swedish and Irish.

Palatone, '039' and the other two numbers, is a particular name: it means *pagnotta grande*, big loaf. In fact, this was the name of the grocery store of the three Cinque brothers. They supplied the whole village. And they often did it 'with the notebook'. In the postwar period and until the early Fifties, there was misery, it must be said. Families took the essentials, then the Palatone would write down the debt, with the date. The family, which generally had some land up in the mountain, would pay, at least in part, this and other outstanding bills, when they slaughtered and sold the calf raised on that land.

Mr and Mrs Petriccioni, '199', are linked to what at the time was a shock for the village. He had a beams factory. They lived at the top of the Sponda, in one of the Gaetani houses. Called '*Bambolina*', babydoll, she used to come to me for hairstyling, always smiling. At one point, she left him. But this wasn't the first time that happened, the fact was that she left him for another woman, a gallerist from Rome. And so Positano learnt before other places that love can rightly also be homosexual.

Tintoriatera	421	Tornatuari	484
		Phome	6807
			85
Taxi			
Michele	317		
	295		

NOME	N.	NOME	N.
Telefono		Barbe TAXS	
H. Amedeo Martino		casa	75359
ufficio Amalfi	871200	garage	75330
casa Marini privato		Giuseppe Fratello	25057
Sille 7.30	44193		

NOME	N.
Zucchi	226
Zambino (Apostino)	209

T
V

NOME	N.	NO
Valli	321	
(Fernanio Piemo)		
081- 986208		

V   WX

The Zucchi, '226', came from Milan, where they had a textile factory. They stayed in a beautiful villa outside, towards Praiano, with a descent to the sea and a goitre. But before they went to the Hotel Savoia, near our coiffeur. Pupa, up here, as soon as she arrived would call me from the street: "I drop my luggage and I'm there!".

Raffaele Castellano, '547', was the tailor. He also sewed to measure, did repairs and similar things. The "Tintoria Elisa", the drycleaner, '421', is still there. It hasn't changed since the Sixties. Now the son runs it. And Taxi Michele, '317', is my first husband. The number was my brother-in-law's, a phone they had in the garage for clients. The Zucchi then, at '226', had a house outside Positano, towards Praiano, a lovely villa with a descent to the sea and a beautiful goitre. But before taking it, they used to come to the Hotel Savoia, near our salon. Pupa, a gorgeous, always cheerful woman – the one who had me make the elegant shoes – as soon as they arrived, would call me from the street: "I drop my luggage and I'm there!".

Anyway, those were the best years I've lived, because Positano was like a magical bubble, those who used to come here forgot about everything else. If she were still with us, my sister Luisa would say the same thing, as on many others I have told. This storytelling, I would have liked to do it together. Regrettably, she left us in 2008, too early. Now, however, tourism has changed a lot, perhaps also because some landmarks have disappeared, such as the Bar Internazionale of Mimì Collina, a character full of warmth and kindness, which had remained the corner where the last affectionate would take refuge. My daughter Maria told me that she and her friends instead enjoyed the terrace of Bar De Martino, at Punta Reginella, after closing. In the dark, with drinks in paper cups, so Ciro could go to rest: he would wake up at dawn, while them, without school, could sleep late.

I have many relatives in North America, in New York. When they came here, they were fascinated, and they come back every year. As I have already recalled, it was my grandmother Flavia that brought many of my family to the United States. She had a beautiful nickname, they called her 'Fravulella', small strawberry. But she was strong and intrepid. Sister of Salvatore Rispoli, who created the Buca di Bacco, she didn't settle for the village life. She was in love with America and was always going back and forth with the ship, living for long periods in New York, along with many other relatives. There is a large Positano community there, they left in 6,500 and had children and grandchildren there. They even celebrate our *Madonna*, every year. She however had fallen in love in Positano and got married here, to my grandfather. Who, on the other hand, was not so fond of travelling.

'Fravulella', nevertheless, started going anyway. From there, she then sent packages loaded with food. She brought there also her adult children, at least the ones who wanted. My mother said no, she fell in love with my father, and got married here. But grandma made that trip twenty-five times. She often took charge also of carrying other Positanesi's children by ship. Boys and kids that their parents decided to send to the United States to let them have a better life. She would take the assignment out of kindness towards her acquaintances, and the boy was left under her protection. Parents paid the journey ticket, often by mortgaging their properties. Houses on which everyone, it must be said, tried not to pay taxes anyway. The system was simple: the doors and fixtures were ripped off, so you could claim to have a ruin.

Pianist Wilhelm Kempff, here beside, discovered Positano in 1928. At Casa Orfeo, created by him, young pianists learn Beethoven. They are next to me, I hear their end-of-season concert from my house. At the top, an edition of "Positano rewards the dance - Léonide Massine" at the beach, in the Sixties.

My grandmother Flavia Rispoli was in love with America and was always going up and down by ship. She lived for long periods in New York, along with several other relatives. She also carried to the United States many of her adult children, who then remained there. Beside, she is in a group photo taken during a crossing, sitting in the front row in a light shade coat. Last on the right, leaning on the balustrade, is Giuseppe Castellano, one of my uncles, that precisely left with the mother and settled in New York, where he was a barber. It was him the one that brought the first metal hair dryer to Positano.

As for the departing boys, apart from being accompanied by my grandmother, they all had to have someone with whom they were going to stay in America. A point of reference, otherwise the embark was forbidden. Now our American relatives, nephews and cousins, come to visit and have fallen in love. They especially like the food, the taste of our tomatoes, the fior di latte, saying that everything is different and tastier. They can't accept that their parents, or grandparents, have left this place. Disgracefully, those were years of misery and without any job prospects, while the United States was growing, even if many sacrifices were needed. Everything has changed now, with the sacrifices we've done here too.

Near where I live, in the greenery, there is Casa Orfeo, of the Cultural Foundation dedicated to the memory of the pianist Wilhelm Kempff. He discovered Positano in 1928 – just a simple fisherman's village, then – and kept coming, until in 1956 he had Casa Orfeo built, and from the following year started there his school for exceptional pianists. Teaching was devoted exclusively to Beethoven's 32 sonatas and five piano concertos, the primary challenge for anyone who wants to tackle the piano. Kempff died in 1991, right here, but the tradition has not been interrupted, brought forward by his most talented former students, who now are teaching the younger ones. So there are still those who come to study Beethoven and at the end of the year there is a concert, which I hear directly from my home.

I have a very nice view in front of me: a splash of the sea where the biggest boats stop and in the evening it is a sight, with their lights on the water. They remind me of the *lampare,* for night fishing, when still part of the village – and of the whole Coast – lived on fishery and not only on tourism. Every night of favourable weather the dark water was dotted with lights like the sky, at the height of the Galli the fishermen would stop – and it formed like a luminous net. Also for tourists, going fishing in the dark was a discovery, another enjoyment. The crew of *Leoni al sole* had become passionate, they went every night off the set.

When I was a girl, many clients told us that we were lucky because we lived in one of the most beautiful places in the world. I could hardly believe it because I didn't know the world very well and I couldn't compare, but then I travelled enough, and I realised: when I get away from Positano, I'm always happy to come back.

I want to conclude by addressing the young people. I hope they realise how lucky they are to have been born and raised in such a beautiful place, and that they will do all they can to protect it for future generations.

ACKNOWLEDGEMENTS

I would like to thank all those without whose help and support this book would not have come to fruition. When it became known in the village that I was looking for images for this memoir of a life spanning decades of Positano's history, everyone who could offered their help, which was particularly needed to illustrate my words. I list them here, adding for each one my gratitude for the helpfulness and affection shown.

Anna Vespoli opened to me the invaluable archive of her husband Luca Vespoli.

Raffaele Scala gave me many of the historical pictures, taken by his father Giovanni Scala.

Daniele Esposito made available to me another historical archive of photographs, curated by him.

Antonio Pane, my nephew of affection, and Vito Fusco, both photographers, also helped.

Other pictures I had from Raffaele Mascolo and from Marianna and Nicoletta Rispoli.

I will never forget my late, dear friend Romolo Ercolino: my heartfelt thanks for the encouragement to keep going that he gave me as long as he could.

I would also like to thank Maurizio Garofalo for his work in selecting the photographs, and of editing, accomplished with professionalism and great patience.

As for Alessandra Baduel, who edited the text, and offered family photos and the address book of her grandmother, I would like to add a thank you for the dialogue established between us and her drive to dig deeper into memories, which has helped me overcome all doubts.

And then there is a special thank you to my son Antonello, who has been with me in this venture since the first day.